Charlie
Washington

7 astonishing methods you can use for improving your relationship

Introduction

Whether you've been dating your partner for a few months or have been married for five years, healthy relationships are built from commitment, mutual respect, and effort. While you probably felt an immediate and effortless spark when you first met, it takes work to maintain that spark as your relationship develops—but don't worry, it will be the most fun and rewarding work you'll ever do. While every relationship is different, you can always work to improve your bond, friendship, and intimacy

Chapter1

With the everyday routine of obligations and frayed nerves, it's reasonable why managing accomplice issues tumbles to the lower part of your rundown. All simply staying aware of life's liabilities — work, kids, family, companions, neighbors, your home — is burdening, and a considerable lot of us are plain drained. Particularly during troublesome times, it's simpler to abstain from confronting your slowing down relationship or dissolved closeness issues.

There are a couple of dependable techniques that work to further develop connections: be a decent audience, cut out time together, partake in a quality sexual coexistence, and evenly divide those troublesome tasks. While these have been demonstrated viable by relationship specialists, you can likewise stretch out to these seven startling ways of holding and upgrade your relationship.

What Is Loyalty?

Part ways

It sounds strange as a method for working on your relationship, yet have some time off from your accomplice. Everybody needs their own space and quality time outside a relationship. Dating and marriage mentors advise us that you merit that space to breathe.

People need time all alone for self-improvement and to keep up with freedom inside the limits of a relationship. While people thrive, the actual relationship benefits. It's vital to fruitful relationships, as a matter of fact.

Whether that implies perusing alone or taking a mobile in the recreation area, make it happen. Or on the other hand perhaps you need to go to an exercise with a companion.

The result is your accomplice's annoying propensities will set off you less. You'll discover yourself feeling revived and being more understanding. Your exceptional has opportunity and energy to miss you, as well.

Different helps: you'll carry more to the actual relationship. Venturing ceaselessly routinely forestalls your time together from becoming old. All things being equal, it takes into account interest, additional intriguing discussions, and development. Basically, taking time separated will spice up the relationship dynamic.

Nod off at the Same Time

Maybe you've proactively perused that most American grown-ups are not getting the seven to eight hours of the evening of solid rest they need. However, did you had any idea that hitting the sack at various times adversely influences you and your accomplice?

For a better relationship, go to bed simultaneously. There are evening people and morning people who live on various timetables, and afterward there are the people who work in bed while the other is watching Netflix in another room. Whatever the circumstance, synchronize your sleep times.

As per Chris Brantner, an ensured rest science mentor, 75% of couples don't head to sleep together, which makes adverse consequences. Those with befuddled rest designs report more struggle, less discussion, and have less sex than the individuals who hit the hay together.

This doesn't give you the approval to jump under the covers and look at your online entertainment while you're both in bed.

Research Shows That Couples Are Impacted By Screen Time

A Pew Research review observed that individuals are irritated by their accomplice's experience on portable devices:1

51% of individuals who are hitched, living respectively, or in a serious relationship say their accomplice is diverted by their cellphone while attempting to talk with them.

4 of every 10 individuals are now and again irritated by their accomplice's cellphone use recurrence.

Be Vulnerable

Now and again you need to dig profound to be powerless. "Couples might think that it is astounding, yet assuming every one becomes inquisitive around one's own vulnerable sides, finds them, and afterward is adequately brave to share that weakness, it can assist with making further closeness," exhorted Meredith Resnick, LCSW, maker of Shamerecovery.com.

Resnick added, "A vulnerable side doesn't be guaranteed to mean a shortcoming or a shortcoming, but instead a profoundly held conviction around oneself or about how a relationship should function, or how love is communicated. The conviction is so profound, we don't understand we have it, consequently the term vulnerable side."

What is an illustration of vulnerable sides in connections? According to resnick, "For instance, one accomplice could find that their propensity to constantly hover over individuals is really connected with their separation anxiety — controlling the timetable of a friend or family member as an approach to never be distant from everyone else.

"Imparting this to an accomplice can be the initial step to changing this example. This ought to be a caring cycle that forms trust, not one that causes disgrace," says Resnick.

Make Novel Experiences

Despite the fact that eating your #1 pizza each Saturday night and consolidating ceremonies in your day to day existence reinforces connections, fatigue creeps in. Consequently, you ought to make a splash — pepper your daily schedule with unusual date evenings and snapshots of tomfoolery.

Going on with immediacy numerous years into a marriage is significant, as indicated by relationship master, teacher, and creator Terri Orbuch, PhD. Her book, "5 Simple Steps to Take Your Marriage from Good to Great," depends on discoveries of an earth shattering review she coordinated that followed 373 wedded couples for north of 20 years. She found numerous life partners felt like they were stuck.

In the event that gutsy dates like stone climbing or learning another dialect are impossible currently, could you at any point purchase a trampoline or accomplish something unforeseen? Perhaps you can track down alternate ways of carrying fervor to your relationship.

Charlie Washington

Clinicians say to zero in on oddity, assortment, and shock. Research shows that following quite a while of fascinating dates, members revived their affection, and the couples felt closer.2

Chapter2

The most effective method to Be Spontaneous in a Relationship

Shock With Little Things

Little motions keep the flash alive and remind your accomplice you are contemplating them. Cheerful couples are caring to one another. Giving or electing to assist is an or more. As a matter of fact, thoughtful gestures are strong, and those that are spontaneous will generally fuel by and large prosperity.

Honor your accomplice's main avenue for affection. For instance, they embrace you since they esteem actual touch. You'd be considerably more joyful assuming they tidied up the lounge room or invested more energy away from their work area, since you esteem demonstrations of administration and quality time together. In connections, figure out how you can show your accomplice your adoration such that your accomplice values.

the Five Love Languages are:

Encouraging statements

Charlie Washington

Quality time

Actual touch

Demonstrations of administration

Getting gifts

Ways Of astounding Your Partner

Carry a cup of espresso to bed

Volunteer to do one of different's tasks

Send a provocative message

Embrace your darling

Meet your adored one at work

Gift your collaborate with chocolate

Leave unmentionables on the bed

Visually connect and effectively tune in

Wrap up a little gift

Pen "I love you" in lipstick on the restroom reflect

Leave a charming tacky note on the front entryway or vehicle directing wheel

Battle Better

While no one needs to contend with somebody they love, conflicts are, as a matter of fact, solid. It's the means by which you battle, and assuming you battle reasonably and usefully, that is important.

John Gottman, PhD, who burned through forty years as a specialist and clinician concentrating on north of 3,000 couples, reveals insight into how to foster a seriously cherishing way of conflicting. The most horrendously awful thing you can do is feign exacerbation or show disdain. Anyway, what works?

Mellow the Start

The accentuation is on your tone and expectation. Talk delicately and tenderly. Courteousness goes far. What's key is to talk without fault. Stay away from a protective or basic comment which can make a contention raise.

Alter What You Say

Try not to proclaim each regrettable idea, particularly when you examine tricky points. Recollect that you love the other and keep up with deference.

Offer Repair Attempts

A maintenance endeavor is an assertion or activity intended to diffuse an argument.3 This could be utilizing humor, contacting the other individual, or offering a compassionate or caring comment like, "This should be hard for you to discuss."

You could likewise figure out some shared interest, such as saying, "Indeed, we have various methodologies, yet we both need exactly the same thing." Or deal indications of appreciation all through troublesome discussions.

Center around the Positives

Sound and blissful relationships offer a rich environment of inspiration. For each bad connection during struggle, a steady and cheerful marriage has at least five positive collaborations.

Thus, attempt to offer five fold the number of positive articulations in your conversations, including your contentions and conflicts. For instance, a blissful couple will say, "Indeed, we really do giggle a ton" rather than "We never have a good time."

Share a Loving Story

While it could astonish you, thinking back can assist with upgrading your relationship. Discussions that beginning with "Recollect when" and journey through a world of fond memories — about your most memorable date, your most memorable home, and entertaining recollections — lead both of you back to positive sentiments. Your accomplice will be helped to remember why they fell head over heels for you in any case.

One more method for fixing and further develop your relationship is to show appreciation for specific characteristics your accomplice has. Continuously add stories to exhibit these astounding attributes.

Since high feelings of anxiety can prompt separation, we will generally zero in on pessimistic stories and what your accomplice isn't doing. In the event that you're feeling neglected, appreciate others. Retrain your consideration on association and positive stories.

These astounding however significant strategies above can assist you with working on your relationship. Strangely, research shows not character or similarity holds couples together. All things being equal, it's the means by which a couple interfaces — how they address one another, how they coexist with one another — and assuming they center around building a relationship together that makes fruitful connections.

Chapter3

Ordinary tips to work on your relationship

Distinguish your profound triggers

Everybody has their "Don't Push" button in a contention — the one subject that can send off us totally into the nonsensical stratosphere of outrage in only seconds.

The explanation that these things hit so contrastingly is logical attached to a past hurt or injury that you encountered.

For instance, say that you grew up with a harmful parent who exploited the other focused parent. Assuming you feel like your accomplice has quit adding to the housework of late, you might end up being lopsidedly frantic in the event that they don't tidy up the table after supper.

Out of nowhere, something moderately irrelevant like a messy table is the platform for a significant battle.

Figuring out how to distinguish your close to home triggers, and all the more critically, why you respond to them, will assist you with improving as a communicator. Self-reflection is critical to anybody's close to home development and the more you can comprehend your responses, the more useful your discussions could be.

Here is a useful introduction on going from distinguishing your sentiments to articulating them.

Know when to yield

Quite possibly of the hardest thing to do during a contention is to pause and divert the concentration. We've all said some unacceptable thing that we wanted to reclaim after we weren't really furious.

Have you at any point drafted a "emphatic" email to a partner in dissatisfaction, yet in the wake of quieting down, removed a portion of the toxin from it prior to raising a ruckus around town button?

Having the option to brake, downshift, and reevaluate your sentiments is an effective method for keeping up with solid social associations, so is there any good reason why you shouldn't matter it to your heartfelt connections, as well?

On the off chance that you're in a contention with your accomplice that is by all accounts getting excessively warmed, check whether there's a chance to hit stop, take a walk, and return to the issue once both of you have gotten an opportunity to relax.

Be interested

Can we just be real for a moment, your accomplice is an exceptional individual to you. Any other way, you could never have decided to accompany them. You were logical attracted to characteristics them that made them captivating. Getting physically involved with somebody implies remaining intrigued and ever-inquisitive about what their identity is and their thought process.

This sort of interest and intrigue can be applied during correspondence as well. While it could be hard to do during a battle, you can take some time subsequently to interface with your accomplice and impartially investigate their decisions and permit them to investigate your point of view too.

Some of the time investigating how correspondence decayed can explore your decisions the following time both of you talk.

Turn into a specialist in sympathy

Quite possibly of the earliest illustration that we get the hang of growing up is to "come at the situation from another person's perspective" since it acquainted you with the idea of compassion.

Sympathy is about something beyond recognizing somebody's sentiments. It's likewise about attempting to comprehend what those sentiments are meaning for their activities.

It's not difficult to neglect to focus on sympathy in the intensity of a contention in light of the fact that your accomplice's perspective disrupts the general flow of yours. In the event that you could make them see it your way, then the contention would be finished. Correct?

This thought process prevents you from showing sympathy since it attempts to just eliminate your accomplice as an obstruction and doesn't stop to address why they were pushing back in any case.

"At the point when somebody feels paid attention to and identified with, they're bound to keep on opening up and share more, which prompts more closeness and closeness generally," makes sense of Hoffman.

"At the point when an individual feels shut down, similar to they are never paid attention to... they will close down over the long run. This can dissolve a relationship and result in exceptionally superficial correspondence and expanded profound division."

Figure out a deeper, hidden meaning

A contention between outsiders is generally two-layered on the grounds that you don't have any acquaintance with them and they don't have any acquaintance with you. One individual savagely mocks, another may rake them over the coals, and afterward it for the most part burns out.

This isn't true for significant others who can bring long stretches of stuff, assumptions, disdain, and history into squabbles. Frequently with couples, what they're squabbling over on a superficial level isn't the thing they are really quarreling over if we somehow happened to dig somewhat more profound.

"It tends to be hard to distinguish what is somewhere beneath contentions about 'insignificant' things," makes sense of Hoffman.

"A large portion of these contentions are about a neglected need, which is much of the time that one or the two individuals feel like they are not being dealt with in that frame of mind... In request to assist with distinguishing what's going on a deeper level, couples need to contemplate what they are truly looking for, and impart that."

Be delayed to outrage, speedy to tune in

During a disagreement, emotions run wild, self images expand, and a fight starts off. A warmed contention can in some cases want to do battle. However, as we race to brace our protections and convey our clear-cut advantages, would we say we are halting to really listen to our accomplices?

While conversing with your mate, returning to old distortions or hold our accomplice's previous way of behaving against them is simple. We could try and lash out once more when we recollect their previous activities.

The issue is that we permit our displeasure to cloud out our accomplice in the present. Regardless of whether they might have acted egotistically before, it doesn't imply that childishness is the thing is driving them today.

At the point when we don't stand by listening to our accomplices, we deny them the chance to be approved and feel cherished. Your relationship can't move into the future assuming you're actually battling somebody from an earlier time.

You realize them best, why not expect their requirements?

For a relationship to recuperate, the two accomplices need to need to pursue further developing their relationship effectively.

Accomplishing the work is difficult, however it's a difficulty that you should outline as a positive test, if not you'll probably be less inspired to continue to work when the relationship hits a hindrance.

You could take a stab at testing yourself by guessing what their requirements are and what they might require from you later on. Assuming you realize your accomplice is going into a difficult week of work, for instance, you can set yourself up for being extra steady during that time.

As a matter of fact, a recent report showed that when an accomplice had the option to clarify what is going on for a mindful, listening accomplice, they were bound to report more elevated levels of fulfillment with their relationship.

If you have any desire to fortify your relationship, don't simply inactively pay attention to your accomplice — let them in on that they're being heard.

"Individuals frequently leap to critical thinking and avoid the sympathy part since they need to fix it," makes sense of Hoffman.

"The expectations are great since it's difficult to see somebody you love in torment... in any case, frequently an individual simply believes their accomplice should tune in and relate."

We should recap

It's feasible to work on a relationship assuming the two accomplices actually trust that there's a compensating organization under all the correspondence breakdowns.

You could attempt to recall what at first attracted you to your accomplice the primary spot and shouldn't something be said about them caught your consideration and energized you. Take that soul of interest and interest into your closeness and disputed matters. You can try to comprehend and cultivate compassion.

You could likewise try to listen to them, stop prior to responding out of resentment, remain in the present, and convey your sentiments, your appreciation, and your statements of regret obviously.

You both have the right to feel approved.

Chapter5

The energy that stems from another relationship can cause you to feel large and in charge. As the originality wears off, the relationship can feel like it's becoming lifeless. You're not ill-fated to stay in a dull and exhausting relationship, nonetheless. There are a few stages you can take to keep an experienced relationship new and invigorating.

1. Keep the Element of Surprise Alive

Shock your accomplice every once in a while in different ways. Get back with a little gift, cook your accomplice's number one dinner or book an unexpected end of the week escape. These sorts of shocks will keep the energy alive and keep you from becoming trapped in a relationship endless cycle.

2. Send Romantic Text Messages

At the point when you're separated, send heartfelt instant messages to each other. This can fabricate expectation for when you'll see each other once more. Use messaging to send short messages of affection, reverence, and consolation. Make sure to send some hot instant messages to zest things up. It is a basic and simple method for keeping the sentiment in your relationship.

3. Plan Regular Date Nights

Most couples go on dates routinely during the underlying period of their relationship. Be that as it may, going out to supper frequently gets exchanged for sitting on the love seat. Thus, the relationship can turn into somewhat dull. Plan ordinary date evenings so you can hang out as a couple.

4. Express Your Loving Feelings

Remember to utilize your words to communicate your sentiments. At times individuals fail to remember that large number of soft things they used to share with each other once the relationship develops. Say, "I love you," frequently and don't avoid words that genuinely express the way in which you feel.

5. Take a stab at Something New Together

Taking part in another movement together can keep the relationship energizing. Take a Chinese cooking class, volunteer at a soup kitchen, or take golf illustrations together. An eagerness to discover some new information can assist you with developing all together.

6. Invest Energy with Other Couples

Investing energy with couples who have sound connections can be great for you. Search for couples who share your qualities and who have serious areas of strength for a. It can assist with supporting the significance of responsibility and assist with reminding you to keep the relationship invigorating.

7. Lay out Goals Together

Make a few objectives that you can deal with all together. It might incorporate a monetary objective, like saving a specific measure of cash to visit on a get-away. Or on the other hand, it could incorporate a wellness objective, like running a half long distance race together. Pursuing your objectives can assist you with feeling like a group and gives you new things to discuss and do together.

8. Examine Your Hopes and Dreams

All things considered, when you were dating, you discussed your deepest desires. Nonetheless, after some time, discussions like that can drop off the radar. Put time to the side to keep on examining your fantasies for the future and backing each other in making those fantasies a reality.

9. Pose Meaningful Inquiries

The kinds of inquiries individuals pose to each other frequently change over the long haul. Questions, for example, "What was your life like when you were growing up?" frequently get supplanted with questions like, "What is it that you need for supper?" Ask significant inquiries regarding your accomplice's past, contemplations on recent developments, and sentiments about various subjects. Attempt to move beyond shallow everyday discussions and jump further.

10. Welcome One Another with Excitement

Chapter6

The manner in which you welcome each other subsequent to being separated can establish the vibe until the end of the day. Making progress with little propensities, for example, the manner in which you welcome your accomplice when they return home, can be critical to an enduring relationship. Welcome your accomplice at the entryway with an embrace and a kiss and express your bliss at being together once more. This can get the ball rolling on the right foot and shown you the way to reconnect subsequent to being separated.

Regardless of how solid your association is as a team, it is critical to keep up with that flash. Without progressing exertion, you and your accomplice could ultimately end up caught in a circle of repeating issues, or living in an exhausting schedule that breezes up dividing you. However, that can be all forestalled assuming you search for little ways of working on your relationship, consistently.

"A sound relationship is one situated in trust and security, [which is why] little signals are an extraordinary method for keeping these two things solid," Dr. Kristie Overstreet, a relationship master and confirmed sex specialist, tells Bustle. Dissimilar to fabulous, clearing motions that happen one time per year, regular, little snapshots of affection show that you're continuously focusing on one another.

It's generally expected in the apparently immaterial minutes that you feel nearest. "For instance, during the business day, checking in with your accomplice, sending them an emoticon, or requiring a couple of moments to visit," Overstreet says.

Ceaselessly trying likewise implies you get to make the kind of relationship you need, Jeni Woodfin, LMFT, an authorized marriage and family specialist, tells Bustle. They offer the opportunity to be deliberate consistently, rather than allowing your relationship to happen to you, after some time.

Chapter7

If you have any desire to remain blissful and associated, recall it's the little moves — the little minutes — that have the greatest effect. The following are 23 methods for making your relationship more grounded, subject matter authorities agree.

1

Use "I" Phrases

In the event that you and your accomplice will more often than not winding into harmfulness during contentions, specialists says you might need to quit utilizing "you" phrases —, for example, "you did this" or "you caused me to feel" — and begin utilizing "I" phrases.

"Driving with the word 'you' almost in a flash makes a guarded stance in your accomplice, who then, at that point, goes into a system to safeguard themselves the moment you hush up,"

"By possessing your own contemplations and sentiments about the circumstance," Dyer says, "you promptly diminish the preventiveness in your accomplice since they aren't feeling accused or scrutinized." And from that point, you can have more useful discussions.

2

Focus On Small Moments

It's not entirely obvious easily overlooked details, such as saying great morning to one another, or embracing prior to hitting the sack. Be that as it may, Woodfin says these are the absolute most significant pieces of the day.

By relishing these experiences, you'll both feel more "seen" and appreciated, which is an imperative piece of remaining associated long haul.

3

Pose Inquiries Instead Of Assuming

Regardless of how well you assume you know your accomplice, it's perilous to make presumptions about the thing they're thinking, particularly during intense minutes. "Mind perusing typically prompts false impressions and put in a terrible mood," Sameera Sullivan, a therapist and organizer behind Lasting Connections, tells Bustle. So whenever you don't know what they need or need, request explanation.

4

Call Time Outs

In the event that you end up in the center of a warmed discussion, and your emotions are raging, make it a point to call a break before things go downhill.

To do as such, just "express the significance of the discussion and the craving to meet up once more," Woodfin says. Something like, "I need to continue discussing this, yet I'm blowing up to think. I will enjoy some time off for 60 minutes, yet we should meet back after that to talk."

That way your accomplice realizes they'll get one more opportunity to be heard, yet solely after you've both allowed yourselves an opportunity to chill.

5

Impart Throughout The Day

Whether it's sending a fast message, or calling to say hello, it is vital to impart consistently. "At the point when you take deliberate minutes over the course of your day to convey, this is a successful method for showing your accomplice that you are considering them," Beverley

Andre, LMFT, an authorized marriage and family specialist, tells Bustle.

6

Share When You're Feeling Down

While you're feeling powerless or upset, try to open up and get in contact with your accomplice, rather than holding everything in.

"Genuine closeness comes from letting your gatekeeper down and permitting your accomplice to observe you in a not exactly heavenly light," Dr. Jennifer B. Rhodes, an authorized clinician, tells Bustle.

Essentially, you can take snapshots of battle or uncertainty, and transform them into a holding experience.

7

Plan Sex

It could sound bizarre, however guaranteeing you plan time for sex — particularly on the off chance that you both tend o be excessively drained toward the week's end — may be the pass to feeling nearer as a team.

As Woodfin says, "With planning sex, you don't need to appear all set, but instead appear with a receptiveness and eagerness to attempt. It's basically the same as that inclination before you go to the rec center — you probably shouldn't go in advance, yet when you finish your exercise you feel perfect, stimulated, pleased. This is exactly the same thing with sex."

8

Plan Regular Date Nights

Likewise, booking standard date evenings is fundamental, Michelle Gallant, a relationship and dating mentor, tells Bustle, if you need to keep major areas of strength for a, association.

It's not difficult to get cleared up with work and different commitments, yet on the off chance that you let the tomfoolery stuff slide — like heading out to the films, getting together for supper, and so on — she says your relationship will begin to disintegrate.

9

Accomplish Something Scary

Perhaps it's climbing in the forest. Or then again performing at an open mic night. Or on the other hand overcoming a feeling of dread toward levels and riding a rollercoaster interestingly. Anything it is, tackle something that alarms you — together.

"We gain proficiency with the most about an individual when they are set in upsetting circumstances; that is the point at which somebody's genuine nature show," Tiffany Toombs, a relationship master and chief at Blue Lotus Mind, tells Bustle.

Furthermore, unnerving minutes offer an opportunity to rehearse critical thinking, Toombs says, which will assist you with feeling nearer as a team.

10

Be Present, Physically

In the event that you feel like you've gotten self-satisfied, put forth a greater amount of an attempt to be physical with your accomplice. "Visually engage, [or] contact your accomplice's arm or leg to tell them you're not kidding," 'Tracy K. Ross, LCSW, a couples specialist, tells Bustle. You could likewise sit nearer on the love seat while staring at the TV, or proposition an embrace. These are simple ways help closeness in your relationship.

11

Check In Regularly

Pick an opportunity to have registrations as a team, whether it's day to day, week by week, or month to month, and utilize this chance to examine the condition of your relationship, Kate Ecke, LCSW, an authorized clinical social laborer, tells Bustle.

During the check in, you could visit about issues, triggers, or beneficial things that have happened as of late, that you'd both like to see a greater amount of from here on out.

12

Keep up with Shared Interests

"In the start of connections, we some of the time track down it exceptionally difficult to avoid one another," Jennifer Weaver-Breitenbecher MA, CAGS, LMHC, a psychotherapist, tells Bustle. Over the long haul, it's normal to float separated, yet you can leave that cycle speechless by intentionally doing more things together.

"Track down shared interests, regardless of whether you're into various things," Weaver-Breitenbecher says. "Or then again find a new thing, something you're both ready to attempt."

13

Sort Out Your "Way to express affection"

Take a test online to sort out your ways to express affection, so you can all the more likely take care of one another's requirements.

"For instance, assuming that your way to express affection is quality time, examine how that affects your accomplice explicitly," Tyra Berger, MSMFT, LCPC, an authorized clinical expert instructor, tells Bustle. What else is there to do — have significant discussions? spend time with you on a more regular basis? — to assist you with feeling adored.

Then, sort out what they need, and do it frequently. "Rehearsing each other's way to express affection will [you] stay associated and on top of one another," Berger says.

14

Alternate

On the off chance that you believe your relationship should feel equivalent, there's a truly basic stunt you can utilize.

"Alternate," Dr. Erika Martinez, an authorized therapist, tells Bustle. "Whether it's arranging night out on the town, cooking, cleaning, or doing clothing, alternating partitions the obligation, makes greater fairness in the relationship, and helps hold these undertakings back from feeling like a weight, which likewise fights off sensations of hatred down the line."

15

Go for A Daily Stroll

Whether you take a stroll in the first part of the day, on your mid-day breaks, or after supper, squeezing 15 minutes of open air time into your day can do ponders for your relationship.

During your walk, "discuss what's functioning admirably in your relationship, what's not working, and what you might want to change," Martinez says. Or on the other hand just clasp hands and visit thoughtlessly about the TV shows you're adoring at present.

It's little customs like these that keep couples close.

www.ingramcontent.com/pod-product-compliance
Lightning Source LLC
LaVergne TN
LVHW020529160826
845677LV00015B/3978

* 9 7 9 8 8 4 4 4 6 5 0 1 7 *